kwabu

There are 30 awesome dinosaurs for you to discover in this coloring book!

We hope you have lots of fun coloring and doodling :-)

Name of the artist

We hope you liked this book! It would mean a lot to us to receive feedback in form of a rating on Amazon or via e-mail at booksbykwabu@gmail.com.

Don't forget to scan the QR-Code below or visit kwabu.com to download your free coloring book!

@booksbykwabu

@booksbykwabu

THANK YOU!

:-)

ISBN: 979-8453827459

Imprint:
Kwabu LLC
Attn: Wes Holmstrom
PO Box 1023
Refugio, TX 78377

Made in the USA
Las Vegas, NV
30 November 2023

81775477R00037